My Thoughts

By Courtland Morrison

Printed in the United States of America

CA Morrison Publishing

ISBN 978-0-9996128-3-5

www.courtlandmorrison.com

Table of Contents

Acknowledgments

First I thank my Father in heaven for granting me this talent.

My parents, my brother, and entire family thank you for your continued love and support.

To all my friends and military family thank you all for supporting my writing career and for giving me a chance to share with you my unique blessing!!

To Creative Expressions Literary Services for the editing, book cover, and promotional graphics for my book. I truly thank you.

Courtland Morrison

My Storm

I feel an uneasiness in my mind

Yet I have thoughts of love, compassion, and
darkness

So many random thoughts I feel discouraged

I feel loved, I feel enraged, I feel humiliated

I don't know why these thoughts torture my mind

From desperation to joy I feel my mind

has been split into two

Yet I know I must keep my faith and pray

That I will get better one second, one moment,

one breath at a time

My storm my thoughts my mind

What is My Path

What is my path?

I have always gone the path of tradition,

hard work, and loyalty. Yet I can see the

path of destruction on my heels.

Trials and tribulations are always ahead

but I see the future of boundless joy

over the mountain tops. The path of destruction

so cold and easy to slide into. Careful

steps and focused concentration brings

me a level headiness which controls my

faith in the most high and gives me comfort.

The divine path is a marathon and the joy I feel daily.

The divine path I try to walk every day.

☐

My Hometown

My hometown my community

The town that developed and molded me

The town that is filled with a love that inspires

The town that prides itself on work

The community that has so much love and blessings

The community is centered around family

The community that gives endless rewards

My hometown is the epitome of love, and friendship

My hometown has shaped many lives and given
service to our nation as a whole

My hometown my community

The town that has developed and molded me

Strong roots, fellowship, and love

Taylortown the community I call my hometown

Queen of Soul

To the queen of soul, you have honored

us with your presence

You have given us universal themes about humanity

The themes of love, respect, and pride gives us joy

The joy of being relatable to each other

The joy of woman being herself and not

the status quo

The joy of having and demanding respect

You have given us these themes

These themes are a blessing from our savior

To give you a voice that would transcend

time but bring people together

So many ways to convey you brought a

heart of gold each and every day

Now Ms. Aretha Franklin take your place by our

savior as he welcomes you in

That voice is the vernacular trademark he gave you

Sing upon the many angels in the glorious heavenly

choir

Sleepless Nights

Precious nights are not a part of me

Only soreness and pain greet me

The struggle I go through is common for me

There are many reasons why I feel this way

PTSD is a menace which we all know

Depression is a puncher that gives doubt

Anxiety is how it comes together

3 to 4 hours is what my body demands

More than 4 hours is a gift that I serenate to

Those few hours are my rest before the

start of work for the day

Sleepless nights a struggle they are

Yet for those few hours of rest I

welcome and become refreshed

Sleepless nights I indulge everyday

I Dream

I dream

I set my mind free

I aspire to set the world on fire

I look to the heavens and seek out

galaxies to dream of my new home

I dream of a new land and new

world to bring a new conscience

O close my eyes and pray I see what the Lord has
purposely built for my path

The door which was closed another has been opened

His grace and mercy are so evident

I humbly oblige the dream

I dream

I set my mind free

I aspire to set the world on fire

I dream

My Father

My father, the man who made me

My father who encouraged me to

explore and gain self confidence

My father who taught me right from wrong and
showed me how repercussions

can mold you and break you

My father who taught me how to be a

gentleman and how to treat a

woman and show respect at all times

My father the role model and the man

I patterned myself after

My father who taught me,

molded me, and chastised me

Though I felt angry at times I now understood the
tough love he gave me to be a leader not a follower

Have my own mind and convictions

Those lessons were not wasted but they were
cherished and fill me with pride today

I thank my Lord and savior Jesus Christ for giving me
my father and blessing Jackie Morrison his two sons
Courtland and Byron Morrison

that will continue his legacy

My Vision

My vision the physical blessing which the

Lord gives us to see

Light , darkness, square, and parallel

Animals, trees, oceans, and rock formations

These physical interpretations are so magnificent they
draw your attention and imagination in your

mind to another view

Yet the Lord also has given us a spiritual vision

Which we cannot see with the naked eye

This vision is the faith we have in our Father in
heaven

We say have faith the size of a mustard seed

The size so small yet the gravity is so great

What a blessing it is to have both

My physical vision to see our Gods' magnificent
works

The faith of our spiritual vision which is bound to our
soul

My Eye for Someone

My eye time of love

Essence and time is the blessing of my soul

I see your strengths and weakness

Baby please leave the stress to the side

I will help alleviate where I can

I know it's hard to but hold on to my word

The essence of love will be your tranquility

Your beautiful brown eyes speak of your spirit

Your voice is soulful and joyful

You are the serenity of my heart, gentleness of your soul

Emotionally I see your strength

Through your children your pride is displayed always

Essence and time is strength for eternity

Timeless beauty forever in my eyes

I admire you so

My diction is my pen from the heart

The beat of rhythm and uniqueness of my soul

The strength of millions transcribed to written epiphany

Lust, passion, and strength develop

Love, compassion, and charity stirs

Friendship and family occurs

The honor in my heart the lover in my soul

Diction forever flows in my mind

State of my mind infinitely revolving

A writer's state of mind

Easter 2018

My blessings are many, yet my thoughts are on my savior

He sacrificed so much I humbly worship him

His reverence I cannot imagine

He dies on the old rugged cross with a thorns as his crown

He is stabbed in his side

What a blessing it is for my Savior to tell his father

They know not what they have done

The third day he rises and beholds he is not dead but alive

He has risen, He has risen

What a day to say thank you Lord for accepting my sins

He only asks if you believe in your heart to take him as your Savior he will grant you eternal life

My blessings are many, yet my thoughts are on my savior

He sacrificed so much how much I humbly worship him

Why I am Vilified?

Why I am vilified, why am I frowned upon

Why as a man of color I am vilified

Why am I looked at with a side eye

Do I give off an aura of fear

Do I represent death and evil

Do I bring shame with my appearance

Why have I been given this scope

Please tell me what I must do to shed this
interpretation

My skin color is brown which has the trait of melanin
to help protect me from the sun

My eyes have many variation of hues which captures
the windows of one's soul

My knowledge is universal and intellect worldly that
my ancestors designed many inventions that are used
today

Yet throughout history I am continually

Vilified as being evil, shameful, and destructive

Why must I be vilified , why I am frowned upon

Why as a man of color I am vilified

Why am I looked at with a side eye

I will not be vilified no more, I will see myself as the

Strong and intellectual man I have envisioned

My bloodline from my parents gives me resolve for
they show me what my heritage is

I will rebuke this perception of vilify into one of
strength and reverence

I will be vilified no more

Changes

Pieces of my heart, struggles with my thoughts

I feel anger and resentment, yet I can't express my feelings outwardly

The guilt and hostility are mind-blowing

My temper flares from my nostrils

Yet through the darkness must come light

A light that fills the dark void and nullness

A light that brings happiness and truth

In my mind I spayed these dark thoughts

I must perpetuate a clear vision of mercy and salvation

I must achieve, I must climb, I must walk

Into the light and away from the darkness

Be mentally strong

Absolve my mind of anxiety, depression, and dark thoughts

Realize my true passions which is positive and love

I must change starting now to achieve the new me

I must not be scared to open new doors and

Jump at new opportunities

I must remind myself of positive thoughts

That will help carry me, go with a trepidation a sense
of urgency

We all have struggles but if we keep positive thinking
we can deal with negative thoughts and banter always☐

The Allusion of YourEyes

The allusion of your eyes personifies me

The beat of my heart flutters of emotion

The delicate balance of love and lust

Your physical attributes are the small details

Which men talk about and lust for

Your mental attributes what real men see

These mentals I want to build a foundation, unify,

develop a family with

Emotions run high and vision can be blinding

That woman a man seeks a man looking for his

queen

The struggle of beauty and passion

The allusion of my eye's personification

of my past leading to my beginning

Epiphany of my heart lover of my soul

The destiny I seek

Friend for a lifetime

A beauty she evokes to me at all times

The Moonlit Sky

I look at the moonlit sky

I began to compose my thoughts

How is the stars and moon defined?

Are they defined by the small reflection of light?

Are they defined by the size and what it's made by?

Are they defined by the geometric shapes they fall in?

So many questions about our galaxy our solar system

What is it that makes me wonder and ponder my
mind

I gaze , astonish, amaze, what and epic sight to
behold

The moonlit sky I question how is it defined?

Defined and seen but answer is to big and to small

Your spiritual eyes can only answer

The moonlit sky

About the Author

Courtland Morrison was raised in North Carolina. He developed a hobby for writing poetry in middle school. He joined the Army National Guard and served honorably doing 2 combat tours to Iraq. During both deployments, he would write for fellow soldiers to help cope with combat and the stress associated with it. He graduated from DeVry University in 2016 with a B.S. in Technical Management. He is currently a Graduate Student attending Keller/DeVry University pursuing an MBA in Global Supply Chain Management. Courtland has always dreamed of becoming a published author and sharing his extraordinaire gift with the world. Courtland is the author of two poetry books entitled First Steps and My Path.